# Stumbling

# Upon My Purpose

## A True Encouragement Story

about finding your purpose in life, fresh ways of parenting special needs children, unconditional love, courage, determination and all the rewards that come with it

# Christopher A. Chaplin

Diana McManus Whitman, Cover art
Dr. Bob Rich, Editor, Consultant
Teodora Sirko, Graphic design
Jan Kovarik, Copyeditor

www.masterpiecefactory.com

Copyright (C) 2006 MasterpieceFactory Inc. &  Christopher A. Chaplin

MasterpieceFactory Inc. 1117 Queen Street West Box 202 Toronto, Ontario M6J 3M9 CANADA

**www.masterpiecefactory.com**

Electronic Collection of Library and Archives in Canada  ISBN# 1-897347-02-2
Library and Archives Canada Cataloguing in Publication   ISBN 13:  978-1-897347-03-4 (English)

First published in English in a paperback edition 2007 by MasterpieceFactory Inc. 1117 Queen Street West Box 202 Toronto, Ontario M6J 3M9 CANADA

**www.masterpiecefactory.com**
**admin@masterpiecefactory.com**

---

Library and Archives Canada Cataloguing in Publication


Chaplin, Christopher A.
Stumbling upon my purpose : a true encouragement story about finding your purpose in life, fresh ways of parenting special needs children, unconditional love, courage, determination and all the rewards that come with it / Christopher A. Chaplin.


Originally publ. in electronic format.
Includes poems.
ISBN 978-1-897347-03-4


1. Chaplin, Christopher A.  2. Parents of autistic children--Canada--Biography.
3. Parenting.  4. Authors, Canadian (English)--21st century--Biography.  I. Title.


PS8605.H359Z475 2007                          C813'.6
C2007-901011-3

# Contents

**Review #1**

**Reviewed by**: Dr. Bob Rich - "The Australian Journal of Counselling Psychology" (number 7(2), page 16) has published a review of my book 'Stumbling upon my purpose'.

I am a professional editor as well as a psychologist. Also, I am a professional grandfather, with a love of children. So, the little editing job I received via email was just right: a picture book for very young children who suffer from handicaps of communication.

The concept and story line were excellent, but clearly this writer was very close to illiterate. Still, I knocked the language into shape for him.

Since that first little book, I have worked closely with Chris Chaplin on a long list of projects: more picture books, chapter books to be read to older handicapped children, the design and wording of his web site www.masterpiecefactory.com (dedicated to helping multiple-handicapped children), and finally, on a book about how he coped with the problems caused by his son's haemophilia and severe autism this book.

By the time Chris wrote Stumbling Upon My Purpose, his use of English was excellent. In his own way, this black man from the ghetto (his own description) is a genius. He is certainly very good at learning, and incredibly creative.

The book starts as a very touching, beautifully written story of how Chris coped with little Christopher's problems, how he developed his own unique approach to doing far more than managing them: he has helped the boy to make gains that The Professionals would not believe. Time and again, Chris defied doctors, educators and other experts, went his own way and succeeded.

But the book is not primarily biography. It is an inspiration and example to others who carry the load of caring for a handicapped child. While it is a sample of one, Chris is careful to point out that it is meant to be used as a starting point in developing a unique approach for a unique child. I think it is brilliant for this purpose.

Many parents despair, feel resentful at fate, and buckle under the strain. Well, all of us are likely to do so from time to time. I am sure Chris has. However, he is a shining example of how to turn adversity into an opportunity for personal growth, giving and love.

The second half of this little volume contains poems and short essays by Chris on a variety of relevant topics, and an outline of the contribution his various other books can make to the education of a multiple-handicapped child.

**Reviewed by**: Jan Kovarik Copy Editor
**Published by**: www.masterpiecefactory.com

My association with the author, Christopher Chaplin, started when he approached me with a request to help him. He had a unique idea about writing children's books, an untapped market for these books, a definite goal…and neither the writing skills nor the money to make it happen. The only true possession he had was passion, and he convinced me to accept the challenge to help him "find his voice." His passion fueled my own passion to become his writing coach, editor, and ultimately his friend.

Stumbling Upon My Purpose is a story about a man faced with having a bi-racial son born with medical and psychological disorders, separation and then divorce from his son's mother, no money, no job, and the discovery that there were no social services available to help him cope with his son's emotional needs. Christopher managed to overcome these adversities by succeeding in creating an environment that is helping his son to overcome autism. It is from this environment that Christopher has created a series of clever and colorful children's books aimed at helping parents of children with medical, physical, and emotional challenges to cope with their own adversities. Christopher not only stumbled upon his purpose, but he also found his voice. It is a voice that is worth listening to.

**Reviewed by**: Frances Savella Honours BSc, BEd, Specialist in Special Education Teacher Toronto District School Board

Stumbling Upon My Purpose is an inspiring and reviting account of a father's relentless will to help his much needy son against all odds. This is a heartfelt story of a father, already struggling with many obstacles including financial burdens, racial issues, an uneventful childhood and a divorce, who gives up his own personal freedoms to enrich his son's life, who is diagnosed with Autism and Hemophilia, through a variety of unconventional methods. It's a story that will teach and inspire anyone who believes "they can't do it."

**Reviewed by**: A.LaRocque-Rooney ECE, CYW, DSW
**Published by**: www.masterpiecefactory.com

Stumbling Upon My Purpose
Is a brief autobiographical account of this parents struggle to cope and understand his child's autism and hemophilia. The author takes the reader through his determination to learn the roots of Autism and the coping mechanisms for both himself and his young son.

This remarkable story is an inspiration for other care-givers to expand their knowledge, and develop much needed coping and teaching skills to help those with Autism and Hemophilia The analogies are sensitive and thought provoking. Several poems speak volumes of the vast emotions and feelings the author has endured.

Parents can take solace in the knowledge they are not alone, that other face similar challenges.

The remainder of this book gives a further detailed view of each of the works written for children of all capacities, each bearing the unique stamp of Christopher Chaplin's personal insight.

A.LaRocque-Rooney, ECE, CYW, DSW

## Comments

Caroline Ganz (parent). says
"You have uncovered the treasure of life - thanks for persevering and revealing this truth to others."

Andree Perreault (ECE and perent of a ADHD child). says
"This book is a true inspiring story of courage, unconditional love and determination against all odds."

Tara Stephen (teacher). says

"Christopher A. Chaplin has filled a niche for the parents, siblings, teachers, caregivers and classmates of special needs children. It was a joy to stumble onto picture books that clearly explain and creatively illustrate the perspective of parent and child. The world of autism, ADHD and other diagnoses can challenge and baffle those who come in contact with them each day. Chaplin's stories are written in such a way as to allow the reader to gently enter this unique world. They are a comfortable read-aloud with plenty of opportunity for discussion at the level of the listener.

Sharing from his own experiences, Chaplin's books are an invaluable educational tool for families and teachers trying to understand the difficulties these precious little ones may encounter in a seemingly ordinary daily routine. Every school, daycare and doctors office should have copies as a gentle way to inform and educate adults, and to sensitively answer the questions of children."

Tara Stephen
-Literacy Co-ordinator & Elementary Teacher with Toronto District School Board
-President of Centennial Child Care Centre Board of Directors
- Mother of three

# Introduction

I AM THE SINGLE-PARENT FATHER OF A CHILD diagnosed with autism and hemophilia. I graduated recently as an early childhood assistant and I am, independently, studying child psychology and children's literature. I am dedicated to bringing to light the positive aspects of parenting children who have special needs.

I have written an abridged version of an inspiring human-interest story that is intended to promote positive parenting and self-betterment methods, both of which are much needed by parents of the rapidly growing autism and other pervasive development and neurological disorders community and all other people who may find themselves in a situation of parenting difficulties.

In this autobiographical story, a man who is experiencing the birth of his son and what should be a tremendously joyful day is suddenly confronted with a situation of emotional tragedy when he learns that his son has been born with the rare bleeding disorder called hemophilia.

The stress of the situation catapults the father into single parenthood and he is forced to endure a difficult court battle for sole custody of his disabled son. While dealing with all the anxiety you can imagine a black man with a less than desirable upbringing would face, the father begins to realize his son is not developing like a typical boy. His child is eventually diagnosed with autism, which adds to the misery and challenges that the man must acknowledge and overcome.

With no cable, Internet, telephone, or established psychology and methods for dealing with these uniquely dire circumstances, the resilient father and his son are forced to exist in a meagerly appointed apartment where, by chance, the father begins to develop unusual learning props and coping devices that prove to motivate the child's stunted development and provide much-needed answers for many of the child's developmental challenges caused by his neurological and bleeding disorders.

In order to further help his son, the father enrolls in a GED (high school equivalency) course and an Early Childhood Assistance (ECA) course; through diligence and determination, he develops methods to further help his troubled child. More importantly, he stumbles upon what he believes is his personal calling in life and his purpose for living.

With the realization that he has discovered unique methods and tools to cope with parenting difficulties, the man's focus is now fulfilling his dream of establishing himself as a writer of children's literature.

While very "personal," my story is written in such a manner as to impart a lesson and to aid parents of physically/mentally/emotionally challenged children by helping them to cope with the situations they face. I am not necessarily saying that my way is the way, but rather I am saying, "Here are examples that you can use to help to 'imagine' coping mechanisms that will work specifically for your child."

This motivational story can encourage parents and people who feel helpless and defeated by their situations and inspire them to overcome their unexpected personal tragedies. Hopefully, this will also help them to find their purpose.

www.masterpiecefactory.com

# Stumbling Upon My Purpose
## *A True Encouragement Story*
Christopher A. Chaplin

"YEAH!" MY NEW CHILD WAS ON HIS WAY. Was I anxious? Sure, but my nerves were soothed by my constant thoughts of parenting a champion, a child who would be admired on the world's stage. However, the delivery did not go as planned and my little Christopher sustained a head injury during birth. Then the doctor marched into our hospital room and announced, "I'm sorry, but your son has hemophilia."

Those words shattered my soul. All my visions of the world watching my son as he raised trophies over his head suddenly vanished. I was attacked by panic and paranoia. Unknowingly, and in spite of my overwhelming disillusionment, then and there I committed myself to intervene in Christopher's life, to help him in any way that I could. I didn't realize then what a commitment this would become.

I guess I was naïve about how our lives would proceed--after all, the last thing one would expect is for parents to separate in a time of shared tragedy. Just when most couples would find a reason to bond and create a strategy for how to succeed together, my relationship with Christopher's mother dissolved. She wasn't ready for the commitment of raising a disabled boy and I was catapulted into single parenthood. My son and I would have to fight our battles alone.

\*

BEFORE CHRISTOPHER'S ARRIVAL, I HAD BEEN working on my dream of being a professional golfer. I was 30 years old and trying to make the cut for the opportunity to qualify for the provincial public championship. Before that, I'd attempted and was forced to abandon two other enterprises. These failures fueled my depression, which was then further flamed by Christopher's birth, and resulted in my personal devastation over my son's situation.

Instead of being bitter about my separation and being left to solely manage my son, I chose to recognize that Christopher's mother is only human. Like most new parents, she prayed for a perfect child; being shackled to a disabled child wasn't part of her plan. In the end, she simply wanted out and I wanted custody and support for my child. Hesitantly, I took this matter in front of a judge.

My lawyer advised me that "all things being equal, custody usually goes to the mother." I began to realize all the many obstacles that you can well imagine that a black man from the ghetto who is suing for custody of a bi-racial, medically disabled child would encounter. Despite all this, I rolled up my sleeves to fight for my life and that of my son, and, ultimately, for my purpose for existing. I vowed not to allow the stress of the upcoming court's decision to cloud my focus on raising my son.

*

OKAY. I HAD TO BEGIN THE PROCESS OF RAISING and caring for my son as a hemophiliac, so I started out with what the doctors told me about Christopher's condition. "Any physically vigorous activity, during which your son's feet can simultaneously come off the ground or cause him to fall, will be considered high risk." What could I do for my child to help him prepare for the anxieties of life as a hemophiliac?

I searched inside myself for answers. I began to see Christopher as an artist, maybe a philosopher… there are many options for someone who can't be physically active. Instantly many new visions and ambitions for what Christopher could become started to emerge.

I began, as any parent would, to stimulate my son's senses with the typical baby games of peek-a-boo, A-B-C, and 1-2-3. But I started to comprehend that Christopher was struggling with what should be a natural learning process. He banged his head and gouged at his eyes to the point that I thought I was doing something wrong. He wouldn't respond to my goo-goo faces and ga-ga noises.

He refused to be bathed. And most discouraging, he would slap at and bite me. When I took him to the hospital for his hemophilia-related prophylaxis program, he was always the last child to receive treatment because he becomes violent around people. He acted like a miniature raging bull.

*

I BEGAN TO RECOGNIZE THAT CHRISTOPHER'S development was not typical for a child his age. He had difficulty with looking at people, smelling and tasting foods, touching things, and hearing new sounds. Everything was a challenge for my son. I asked the doctors questions about these behaviors, but with all the other issues surrounding his bleeding disorder, they were only willing to advise that I "wait and see." And truthfully, even if I'd heard it at that time, my pride would have refused to accept the fact that Christopher would be diagnosed as being autistic.

*

FOR THE FIRST FEW YEARS, EVEN THOUGH Christopher couldn't say more than Da-Da, Up, and No, I disguised my concern about his severe speech and language deficits. I parented Christopher diligently and did my best to brush off and, worse, to cover up the fact that by three years old, he could only say a handful of words with any clarity.

At the age of three he was, in many ways, still acting like an infant. His self-injurious behavior, severe speech and language impairment, and cognitive and social-emotional difficulties could no longer be ignored by the doctors. Even though my early efforts alleviated some small measure of Christopher's problems, his medical history and social conditions led the doctors to the diagnosis of autism and once I spent endless hours researching the many signs and symptoms of neurological disorders and contemplated all that I had gone through with him up to this point, I both realized and accepted that Christopher was not just autistic, he was severely autistic.

*

FOR AN EXCRUCIATINGLY LONG FRACTION OF a second or two, I felt that I was doomed, life was over, and my son and I were now hopeless. But then a brief glimmer of common sense warmed my eviscerated spirit and allowed me to realize that the diagnosis of autism was actually a major upgrade from having doctors tell me that my son was irreparably brain-damaged. I decided that I would think of my son's flawed little brain as a lump of clay that needed only to be lovingly and precisely shaped and formed into a working, functioning brain. And so the process of evolving my ideas for doing just that began.

I became accountable for my son's situation and continued to research neurological disorders. I soon realized that Christopher's insatiable desire to watch things spin, his lack of receptive skills, his unusual fear of people, places, and things, along with his way of walking on his toes, stacking things on top of each other, memorizing sequences and precise orders of events and being fastidious were all the result of his neurological disorder.

*

IT WAS ALMOST A BLESSING FOR ME THAT WE were stranded in our shabby apartment. Our lives were extremely unstable and inconsistent. My memory grew erratic, my hair fell out, I aged visibly, and my eyesight, hearing, and overall health declined. Although my son, for the most part, lived in his own little world, I had to contend with the day-to-day struggle of just trying to provide adequate food, shelter, and the exacting care that Christopher required. His anxieties made it impossible for me to work or leave his side, and eventually, my loving mother was forced to take out a second mortgage against her property so that I had some much-needed financial resources.

I had to accept that this was how life would be for some unknown stretch of time and I fought (and still fight) to shield my son from my angst. Every day was a scary experience for us, but with the help of my mother and my "Father, Who Art in Heaven," (Who is God) we managed to make it through each day.

\*

EVERYWHERE I WENT, CHRISTOPHER WAS in my arms. Going to the grocery story was (and is) a grand activity, even though many times I was forced to replace cans and boxes that Christopher swiped off the shelves. I never miss an opportunity to lift my son in the air and cheer, "Yeah, you did it!" when he makes eye contact with others or appropriately responds to conversation. People don't understand this spontaneous hoopla, but it is what I do to help my son move forward.

*

WHEN CHRISTOPHER HAS A TANTRUM IN public, I explain matter-of-factly to whomever is staring, "My son is autistic." The typical response I receive is, "He doesn't look autistic." I smile, but inside, my soul is provoked by their ignorance of what I have to go through every day. Nevertheless, my determination to deal positively with Christopher's situation helps others to become more sensitive toward Christopher and autism, while educating their perception about Pervasive Development Disorders. I have, for the most part, become desensitized to Christopher's outbursts…but not completely. My son does find new ways to challenge my nerves while we are in the public eye.

*

SOME OF THE CASHIERS AND STORE STAFF, AS well as the people who frequent the places we regularly visit, have joined in on my "Yeah, we did it!" crusade. They tell me details of friends who have autistic and other difficult-to-parent children. They usually tell me that those children are not doing as well as Christopher. I empathize with these parents; they most likely must go to work and leave their children in the care of others, allowing them to quietly spin in circles or stack toys in a less than emotionally supportive environment. Although we have very little, I am able to be at home with Christopher and provide spiritual stability. Furthermore, I am dedicated to diligently working with my son and managing his therapy myself.

I have determined that it is this constant comfort and compassion that is helping Christopher to make his inexplicable but noticeable improvements.

My dire circumstances forced me to involve my child with the total process of how I live--and he began to live through me. He started to open up to life and openly crave information like a hungry man craves food. He began to understand the process of wanting something, and he learned very quickly the "politics" of getting what he wanted. He is much like me; he wants to observe and experiment with everything, and he wants to know things. He wants to learn, but it is so hard for him to understand even the simplest things most times.

＊

HOW DO YOU TEACH A CHILD WITH neurological abnormalities?

How could I teach my child new things in a way that he could comprehend them? How was I to be a father, provider, and teacher of a child who is both emotionally and medically challenged? I finally determined that the only way to accomplish anything was to confront Christopher's innumerable anxieties head on. And so, the learning process began--both for him and for me.

Being an unemployed, undereducated, single, black father of a child with special needs who was in the midst of an ugly court battle and facing what seemed to be insurmountable odds left some child care professionals with doubt about my ability to manage my son's autism. Their suggested methods were intended to help me cope, but nothing more than that. I didn't need, or want, that type of help. I wasn't interested in just surviving. I was looking for tools to help Christopher and me thrive. With no answers available and no known cure for autism, I had the incentive to put my heart and soul into finding answers for Christopher.

*

IT WAS NOT WHAT I HAD ENVISIONED FOR myself, but I had stumbled upon my purpose in life and proceeded to search for answers full-steam.

I was convinced that, through Christopher's success, I would also succeed. Furthermore, I wanted to be a role model for my child, but how was I to become the type of role model he needed? What could I become that would ultimately benefit us both? What could I do for my own self-esteem?

I felt abandoned and discouraged by my son's previous pediatrician and speech therapist. I decided that my only hope was to search within myself for the answers I needed.

I had to find or invent some way of helping my son overcome the tremendous hurdles that life had put in front of him. My son is bi-racial, autistic, a hemophiliac, and can be self-injurious. He is hyperactive, has numerous sensory issues, and suffers from major speech and language difficulties. With all the above-mentioned unique personal and professional challenges I have, there was no formula, no established psychology, and no accepted methods for dealing with our situation.

I had to take a hands-on approach. I needed to become a teacher and I needed to learn more about child development, so I knew I needed to further my own education.

*

I NEEDED AT LEAST THE EQUIVALENT OF a high school education to enroll in the necessary classes. I knew what I needed to do. I enrolled in both a GED course and an Early Childhood Assistant (ECA) course. Like Marshall Mathers , I knew I'd only have one shot at this, and I couldn't afford to drop the ball.

Trying to study with my son on my lap was an enormously frustrating task. I soon realized my efforts and the forced composure I exhibited while researching questions and formulating answers became an exercise and a tremendous tool for me to use for my son's development. He learned how to learn by watching me and playing observation games.

I began to point and tell and he began to ask "What?" and "Why?" by listening to me talk aloud while I studied. My enthusiasm for my schoolwork made him enthusiastic. I believe my ability to accept the challenge to better myself and to follow through also empowered him.

By the time that I'd successfully completed my courses, I had to face the fact that Christopher was actually regressing in the preschool class (not at the fault of the staff) in which I'd enrolled him. I decided to home-school Christopher and test my new knowledge and skills--after all, nobody knows my son better than I do. I developed new ideas and Christopher feels most comfortable and safe learning through me. Home-schooling Christopher paid off.

*

*"Let Them Be Silly So They Can Become"*
Christopher A. Chaplin

**www.headitchy.com**

I WAS ABLE TO WORK WITH HIS SILLY behaviors and he was able to learn though my eccentric teaching techniques and, in turn, he allowed me to help him move forward. I accelerated Christopher's development because we worked together in a manner that he could mentally accommodate.

Because of his self-injurious behavior, Christopher could not actually "be taught," so I took the approach of "training" him. During his initial psychological assessment, the evidence of Christopher's history of autism was borne out. His receptive language skills scored as "severely in deficit" and much lower than his expressive language skills deficits, which were moderate to severe, as well.

He could ask for what he wanted by pointing and his reflexes allowed him to appropriately respond to some basic activities he was shown, but he had no clue about or apparent ability to understand common verbal or nonverbal language commands. For instance, a typically developed person would have the ability to go to a foreign country and get by, however marginally, on simple sign and body language alone. Christopher experienced difficulties interpreting even the most basic hand signals and verbal commands, like waving your hand toward yourself to indicate "Come here."

Christopher had no idea how to express and understand the English language without banging his head and flapping his hands in a tantrum. I worked on training his brain to respond and act appropriately to the common cognitive signals a toddler's growth chart would suggest by speaking and pointing, and then reinforcing my language commands in whatever way worked for him. We developed our own little cues (and hand gestures) like giving Bumps (touching fists together) to break the ice with someone new. These inventions helped Christopher move forward.

WHEN CHRISTOPHER TURNED 4, AND AGAINST teachers' and therapist's recommendations, I made the decision to enroll him in a typical kindergarten class (of about 24 children). After an in-classroom assessment of his developmental status, it was suggested that Christopher should stay in a preschool class where he could receive much more support as he was still very behind in his language and social development, including behavioral problems.

I refused the thought of him being held in a preschool environment with younger children, most of whom had difficulties of their own. This wouldn't provide Christopher with the role models that he needed to help him to improve and mature.

\*

I COULD NOT SEE HOW THAT ARRANGEMENT COULD benefit my autistic child, other than the fact that it would give me a few hours each day to think by myself. Ultimately, I made the decision to remove him from any type of daycare program and continue to home-school him. For us, it was, indeed, the School of Hard Knocks.

A few weeks later I was notified that Christopher was invited to enroll in a special education program. I thought that in such a program, Christopher would receive special attention. Instead I received phone calls that he wasn't responding, he was "acting tired," he was "too sensitive," too hyper, and too afraid, and after he sustained a second bleed while there, I removed him from that class as well. We would go back to home-schooling--but how could I teach him, past a preschool level?

At first it felt as though I was spending all of my time in just managing his spirit, and keeping him on an emotional even keel. Everything I did for him seemed simple, too simple to be helping him move forward. But in time, I perceived that the unconventional learning and coping props that I'd developed were facilitating his development and allowing him to be more receptive to life. I used my imagination and kept my mind open to use and do whatever worked to help him, regardless of how outlandish it seemed. After all what choice did I have?

This was far from a conventional circumstance; I was forced to compromise my methods to suit my circumstances.

*

CHRISTOPHER'S AUTISM MEANT THAT, FOR him, every day was an unknown. Autistics seek sameness and repetition and, at first, I worked hard at doing everything exactly the same, every day, because I knew that would help prevent his self-injurious episodes. But I began to cave in from the stress of trying to provide Christopher with precisely the same sequence of events, under exactly the same conditions every day. I also began worrying constantly about money, and not being able to control even simple things like when I ate or slept. Christopher's erratic behaviors made me erratic as well. I came to the conclusion that sameness would only keep my son in the same place where he existed, physically and mentally.

I did not want Christopher to stay the same; I wanted Christopher to be prepared for life's constant changes.

My personal circumstances outside of Christopher were attacking what resolve I had left. It was difficult to not have a quiet place to escape and recoup my thoughts. But I remained responsible for his every move. I had accepted the fact that I was permanently attached to my son and understood the responsibilities I had taken upon myself. My immediate outlook on life, as well as foreseeing any hope for a productive future, was grim. I admitted that I needed someone or something to help me cope with my perpetual pain and anxieties.

*

I COULDN'T FIND RELIEF IN MARIJUANA OR alcohol. Instead of emotionally or physically abandoning my son, I quickly realized why my Jamaican mother always sung to me when she should have been furious; it was to keep her from going over the edge and taking out her personal frustrations on me in the form of physical or emotional abuse. I began coping with my frustrations in much the same way. Instead of shouting and screaming at Christopher, I rapped, sang, jived, and acted silly. Soon all thoughts of anger would be disguised by the face of laughter and, yes, I must thank the powers that prevented me from succumbing to drugs and alcohol and any other deleterious habits that would have kept me from my purpose.

Accommodating Christopher became my "habit" and like any habit, I needed to maintain it. The only escape I had from the constant barrage of his demands was my ECA course, for which I was forced to write and create activities and record classroom experiences in a journal to submit to my teacher. As soon as Christopher fell asleep each evening, I would morph from possessed parent to engaged student. I developed a routine of studying and writing and found solace in both. That course became my savior, and writing would become my voice.

*

I SPENT WHAT PERSONAL TIME I HAD BY BEING preoccupied with assignments and research. I also began to write simple stories for my son, stories that made sense to him. Writing these stories began to liberate me and make me receptive to the thoughts of success, of succeeding in sculpting that lump of clay that was not only Christopher's little brain, but also was his life. I was motivated to actually study my son and diligently parent him with the goal of making every day a learning experience with an opportunity to move him forward, even if only a little. My observations and experimentations had new meaning; they became the source that would fuel a new life for us.

I began to believe that other families in similar circumstances could benefit from learning about what we were doing.

I set out to do the improbable: to help Christopher become whatever he thought possible for himself. I devised my own incentives for coping with and, more importantly, learning how best to manage my son's difficulties in the manner that works best for us. I developed a method for employing what I'd learned in a manner that would help Christopher to learn, grow, and begin to mature. I want us to beat autism. I want to be able to shout, "Yeah! We did it!"

*

I BEGAN TO MAKE A POINT OF OBSERVING Christopher's patterns of being exposed to new things and how he attempted to digest those new experiences. I studied his capacities for learning, how much he could absorb without becoming overwhelmed and retreating into his self-injurious modes. I experimented with new ideas (and attitudes) about how to integrate Christopher with people, places, and things.

I implemented my methods of teaching Christopher and also worked at keeping him in touch with what we'd already learned. I circumvented his autistic tendencies by holding him in my arms or having him ride my shoulders when we were in busy places, where there would be many new people and things that he would have to assimilate. I allowed him to develop his language skills and overall ability to open up to life by surrounding him with exotic pets (Snakes, Parrot, Spiders)that would normally scare most children his age (certainly most adults, too). He observed them in fear, but soon was handling them. He learned to sense when they were hungry, afraid, or ready to breed. I would ask him questions and he learned to ask me questions, too. Soon his perceptive motor skills began to improve. In many ways, Christopher's severe liabilities developed into some extreme abilities.

*

WE CONTINUED TO WORK ON HIS MANY OTHER    autistic tendencies, primary of which was his self-injurious behavior and required him to wear a helmet whenever we went out. The helmet drew attention to Christopher, and created an anxiety level that, for both of us, was difficult to handle. With observation, experimentation, and perseverance, I was able to help Christopher overcome the majority of this hurtful behavior, to the point where he can now go out without needing to wear his helmet.

In time, everywhere we went, people showed shock at Christopher's drastically improved presentation. He was enthusiastic and high-spirited; he began to speak and although he had trouble relating to other people, he began to show willingness to interact with other children. He became interested in being exposed to new people places and things, and he stopped banging his head at every unexpected turn.

With the custody battle burning strong and Christopher's mother's camp trying to "make all things be equal," it did not help my case or emotional state that some professional caregivers downplayed my accomplishments with Christopher. The fact remains, however, that he is developmentally delayed and that Christopher is making progress and is beginning to overcome many of his autistic behaviors. Despite their criticism, I continued on as I knew Christopher and I were exceeding our own expectations. And, like Pinocchio, Christopher has begun to learn and grow and become a real boy who, I hope, will some day be a genius.

*

*"Autism is like the wind; it is invisible. You can see its effects, but you can't see autism itself."*

Christopher A. Chaplin

**www.headitchy.com**

THIS IS NOT TO SAY, HOWEVER, THAT Christopher is "normal." He still cannot do normal childhood things like blow his nose or independently button up his pants or shirt. He still has problems relating to other children and people, his speech is hardly pragmatic, he is still fastidious, and he continues to attempt to injure himself during transition period, at sudden changes or when he perceives the slightest disapproval.

Christopher still must deal with his severe hemophilia, which is always a contentious situation that worsens as he becomes more physically capable of putting himself in harm's way. And my overall personal circumstances have not improved; I am burnt-out, which adds to the turmoil of our life.

I learned to draw some measure of strength from other parents who congratulated me about Christopher's progress. They talk to me about their family members and friends who have developmentally challenged children, and the many difficulties that they, too, face on a daily basis. I began to feel as though maybe, just maybe, I might be able to help them--but how? I did not have time to study exactly how or why I was doing the things I did; I was forced to be spontaneous about everything in our lives. How could I best express just what it is that led me to the techniques I use to teach Christopher? How could I help other parents so that they could help their children?

*

AND THEN IT HIT ME - TELL OUR STORY, AND tell it as a story. I had always wanted to provide my son with stories that would help him, but we couldn't find anything in libraries or stores or on the Internet. I wanted to create stories for Christopher that would not only entertain him, but also stimulate growth through providing a visual understanding of behaviors that he could relate to through his autistic sense of reality. If these little stories could help Christopher, then maybe they could also help other parents cope with their developmentally challenged children. My realizations of my purpose were reinforced and so I began to learn how to write the types of stories that could be universally helpful to us, and others, too.

To write my stories, I first had to look back at how Christopher and I explored and discovered ways to help him assimilate information, to absorb it in meaningful ways. Each day, we also worked on feeding our spirits, as well as creating new ways to accelerate his stunted development.

As I began to write, the stories grew into colorful tales intended to help Christopher remember the lessons and experiences that we have encountered. But my stories were rough and awkward. I was told by established authors that I had a special flair for writing, but I didn't have any foundation in grammar and syntax.

This had some basis in my own hearing deficit in both ears, which prevented me from really developing "an ear" for language and speech patterns. I sought help from writers who had been slaving in the trenches of the conventional writing world for years.

BUT I DIDN'T FIND THE HELP THAT I NEEDED from those critique groups or in various writers' chat rooms. I eventually stumbled upon a copyeditor who was keen enough to invest her time and help me develop my natural writing skills and refine my ideas. She became my coach and I became literally indebted to her. But I'd found my voice.

My stories now capture and reflect the methods that I have used to encourage Christopher's development. They promote the "We can do it!" type of attitude that parents have to take on when dealing with special needs (all) children. My way may only work for me, but it can at least help to motivate other parents to not be afraid to use their own ideas for teaching and moving their children's development forward too. Special needs children do indeed have special needs, and to cope with those needs, we can't be afraid to come up with new ideas, special tools, and to jump outside the box of typical therapeutic methods.

After all, no two families experience autistic circumstances that are exactly the same, so how can there be a conventional method for intervention?

*

AFTER A LONG VICIOUS COURT BATTLE, all parties came to an agreement. I was awarded primary custodianship of Christopher and his mother has now developed a great relationship with her son. But like a marathon runner who finally reaches the finish line, I collapsed; I was left lifeless and my resolve was forced to face the even greater test of turning my life into something that could positively influence the life of my son and others around me.

*

WITHOUT AN ENGLISH DEGREE OR PREVIOUSLY published works, the odds of me becoming a recognized published author were stacked against me. With that realization I decided to work toward developing my own publishing company (to be called MasterpieceFactory ©), which again would not prove easy. With no phone or Internet access at home, my temporary office was the resource center at my local social services office. There I would get a few hours a day to research and send out query letters, manuscripts, and faxes.

It's time now to look after my personal health, continue to work on my son's development, and to begin to promote the notion of positive, productive, and effective parenting methods developmentally challenged and other difficult-to-parent children. I hope to do so through my series of "Yeah, We Did It!" Encouragement Stories ©, which I hope to have illustrated and published in the near future.

Until such time as my stories can talk for me, my advice to parents of developmentally challenged children and all who may feel disheartened is to do "whatever works" for you and your child. Don't be afraid to set lofty goals for your children, and for yourself. Autism and other emotional disabilities may seem invisible to those who don't understand them. Deal with your situation openly and without shame.

You can learn much about yourself through your child and, if you make your child's developmental goals your primary objective, you may stumble upon your purpose and, in turn, provide hope for those around you, too.

To be continued…

*"If your ambitions are to reach for the roof,
you will learn how to climb a tree.
If your ambitions are to reach for the sky, then
you will learn how to climb a mountain."*

Christopher A. Chaplin

**www.headitchy.com**

# ACKNOWLEDGMENTS

I thank these influences on the production of this book, in particular:

- God, my "Spirit in the Sky"
- Patricia Chaplin
- Christopher T. Chaplin II
- Jan Kovarik, Copyeditor
- Dr. Bob Rich (counseling Psychologist multiple award winning author)
- Diana McManus Whitman, book cover/back portrait illustrations
- Teodora Sirko, graphic design, layout/typesetting
- Elizabeth Tytova
- Carlos Dantas
- Lin Wen, B&W Portrait Page 36
- Renai Swan
- Pamela J. Masi
- Jody Felske

# *Poetry & HeadItchy*
## *by Christopher A. Chaplin*

# *HeadItchy ©*
# *Matter that makes you mind*

A HeadItchy © is a hypothesized philosophical saying, poem, phrase, or quote that originates from the author's personal research, encourages the reader to think about its subject matter, and then simultaneously begin the process of justifying its relevance for his or her own life and personal belief system.

HeadItchy sayings are created by Christopher A. Chaplin as an outlet for his philosophical views.

"As a creative writer and independent developmental researcher, I found myself discovering fresh methodologies for managing various life issues and then jotting down multiple phrases, statements, and quotes to be used as subject matter for future literary projects. As I began refining my statements for publishing, I realized that my findings would be better received by the public and more practical as stand-alone literary pieces so that my readers could scratch their heads and accept my thoughts as is or contradict them with their own personal research and life experiences. After reading my HeadItchies, I encourage my readers to write their own."

# Perpetual Statement Of Acknowledgment
(C) 2006 Christopher A. Chaplin

I thank all the people, places, and things that have, are, and continue to obstruct me--without these influences and forced experiences, I could not have recognized and developed the strength, vision, and spirit I needed to overcome the obstacles before me and accomplish my goals in life.

To every entity that has, is, and will contribute its confidence, admiration, and support toward the development of my being--my accomplishments will represent the fruits of your encouragement. Without them, I could not have become nor remain positive, productive, and prosperous in life.

*

# *If We, They Will*

## (C) 2006 Christopher A. Chaplin

If we criticize our children for what they cannot control, they will learn to condemn.

If we educate our children with ridicule, they will become shy.

If we surround our children with hostility, they will learn to fight.

If we discourage our children from developing ideas, they will exist without ambitions.

If we accept our children, they will feel pride.

If we praise our children, they will appreciate life.

If we tolerate our children, they will learn to be patient.

If we are rational with our children, they will understand justice.

If we live with friendships, our children will learn to find love in this world.

The way we choose to exist influences what our children will become.

## *Autism's Address*

(C) 2006 Christopher A. Chaplin

I am a neurological disorder known as autism. My mission is to halt the development of children of many races, colors, shapes, and sizes.

I was set free to wreak havoc in the minds of girls and boys when mothers began supporting their own families and earning their own toys.

I attack the brain and damage all five senses. I manifest mostly in the minds of children who are born with disabilities, disorders, and diseases.

Vaccinations are not the cause of me. My origins are early childhood stress on the brain; my traits can be found in its family tree.

Children cannot protect themselves from their parents' anxiety and stress. I am free to cause disorder and then leave your child's senses in a mess.

Walking on toes, self-injurious behavior, and not making eye contact comes next. Your broken prizes will become permanently dependent at best.

My adoration for my abilities are expressed, when your children can't tell if your sad face is a smile, or when socializing they hide their head in your chest.

Most recently a child may have narrowly escaped me. Teachers and therapists believe he is clear and free. Their ignorance allows me to be imperceptible. Without a forensic approach I will always be invisible.

The child's parent recognized my forces from the onset. Yes the child was born with just a clue, but it was the parent's decision to do whatever it takes to prevent me from turning the child into an adult that says "ga-ga-goo-goo."

The focus is on developing the child's creative, spiritual skills. The parent doesn't sandbag when it comes to parenting or sit around and wait. Their persuasion is to initiate.

The kryptonite is love, diligence, and acceptance; those are the most efficacious strategies to manage me.

The parent demonstrates to his child how to handle anxiety and stress. The child lives in a creative science environment in which self-healing is the best.

If you can look within yourself and become accountable for your little-you, you will find a way to manage autism, too.

*

## *Let Them Be Silly So They Can Become...*
(C) 2006 Christopher A. Chaplin

Our methods of developing our children should sustain our ambitions for them to become admirable on a world-class level.

Our focus should be on developing their special skills, not molding our children to the closest resemblance of what is socially acceptable--for they will not be able to accept themselves.

If our children develop unique talents, they will have the security of social tolerance and praise.

Our children are happy and connected when allowed to be silly. They become angry and disconnected when they feel not accepted.

Our children's impairments, mannerisms, and behaviors may subside in time, but they will always be autistic and autism will always be invisible.

Let our children be silly so they can become…

\*

# *What A Child Is Worth*

(C) 2006 Christopher A. Chaplin

To live is to have self-worth.

To have self-worth is to will for life.

To will for life is to want to live on.

To live on is to want to have a child.

To have a child you must be willing to learn.

To be willing to learn is to have goals.

To have goals you must have patience.

To have patience is to have self-confidence.

To have self-confidence is to be positive.

To be positive is to be productive.

To be productive is to become prosperous.

A child is an idea worth everything to succeed for.

\*

## *Without Anxiety*
(C) 2006 Christopher A. Chaplin

Boom! Bang! Crash! Growls the thunderstorm;

That sinister sound is my cue.

Pitter-patter splatter rain drops;

Significant play time now due.

Splish! Splash! shout the angry puddles;

Yeah I Did it Daddy, thank you.

\*

## *Stage Spook*
(C) 2006 Christopher A. Chaplin

My poem is ready,
Classmates eyeball me on stage,
Tics overcome me.

*

51

## *Autism Is Emotional*
(C) 2006 Christopher A. Chaplin

Autism is emotional
Our emotions control how we think
How we think becomes our action
Our actions become the way of our being
Our way of being becomes the way of our children
When we reject our children and their ways
Our children exhibit signs of autism
When we refuse to expose our children to people, places, and things
Our children's development becomes retarded
We then ask ourselves why…
… I think this is one reason why.

\*

# *People Fear*
## (C) 2006 Christopher A. Chaplin

Sun shine,
Salty breeze
Couldn't
entice the
child to play.

\*

### *Being Or Becoming*

(C) 2006 Christopher A. Chaplin

Without a defined purpose to grow
The self-Esteem of mankind is low.
Choose not to be a mere human being
Exist on this earth to obtain meaning.
In this human race prepare to start running,
Think of yourself as a human becoming.

*

## *The Closer We Get To Our Goals, The Fiercer The Enemy Becomes*

(C) 2006 Christopher A. Chaplin

Inspired By the Words of Diana McManus Whitman

Evil tries to distract us from our goals; it attacks us from every side.

The closer we get to our goals, and to the Lord, the fiercer the Enemy becomes.

We find solace in knowing that when Evil attacks, our goals are our guiding light and the Lord is our strength.

If we are on the right path when Evil attacks, then Evil cannot have us.

If we are on the wrong path, then Evil would not have to attack--Evil would already possess us.

If we are on the right path and make the ultimate sacrifice while pursuing our goals, we will be received by God and encourage others to fulfill our dreams.

We shall be prepared for the anxiety and suffering of pursuing our goals while on the correct path.

We shall fear the misery and persecution of succumbing to Evil and not pursuing our goals.

The closer we get to our goals, the fiercer the Enemy becomes.

# *Where Is Autism*

(C) 2006 Christopher A. Chaplin

Where is autism?
Only its effects we see;
Like the wind it be.


*

### *Express Emotional*
(C) 2006 Christopher A. Chaplin

We Must Be
Whatever we inspire
Our children to become
Express your emotional.

\*

## *May The Thirteenth*

(C) 2006 Christopher A. Chaplin

Every May the Thirteenth is Mothers Day
On this day planet Earth shouts Hip Hip Hooray

For the infinite greatness that Moms do
We reserve this day to say I love you

Without Mothers life would not be the same
Without Mom we could not commence life's game

On May the Thirteenth we salute, cheer and
Execute ideas to make Mothers feel grand

For the often thankless task that Moms do
We honor them for their love that is true

Moms have endless responsibilities
To ensure our possibilities

That's why we dedicate one day in May
To thank our Mothers in our special way

For the relentless work that Moms must do
Whatever we can to express we love you.

\*

## *Problems Needed*
(C) 2006 Christopher A. Chaplin

"Without problems there
Would not be ideas to
Grow; use your mind, think"

\*

## *Toronto To Ancrum*
(C) 2006 Christopher A. Chaplin

Let them be silly so they can become,
Special children prepared for the world stage;
Performers from Toronto to Ancrum.

Develop their gifts or they will succumb
To their autism and develop rage;
Let them be silly so they can become.

Every family tree from Sharum
To Smith has autism concealed in cage;
Performers from Toronto to Ancrum.

Enhance their unique, or they will succumb
Depression from pursuing the same page;
Let them be silly so they can become.

Grow Stratagems for your child to become
Genius despite their challenges or age;
Performers from Toronto to Ancrum.

Even if your name is Mr. McCrum
Promote their gifts and they'll procure a wage;
Let them be silly so they can become
Performers from Toronto to Ancrum.

\*

## *Autism Under Hypnosis*
(C) 2006 Christopher A. Chaplin

I breathe air and require food
I search for friendships and love
I know I am still human
But it's eviscerating to be social

I can read and conceptualize
I may lose control of my body during social interaction
I know I am still human
But I'd rather be home feeding my obsessions

I am not insensitive toward human feelings
I'm abnormally sensitive
I know I am still human
But I'd rather be innovating

Being lost in a parallel crowd is okay
The suffering I sense in people compromises my happiness
I know I am still human
But I'm allergic to the frivolous aspects of social interaction

Instead of accepting what my senses receive
I visualize everything until I believe it's happening to me
I know I am still human
But I have to manipulate my mind to manage social politics

I don't maintain relationships well
My greatness secures human contact
I know I am still human
But I still exist with autism.

### Open Your Mind
(C) 2006 Christopher A. Chaplin


Like skies over mountain peak
Open up your mind
Every answer you seek
Will be there to find.


\*

### *Mute Until Humbled*
(C) 2006 Christopher A. Chaplin

Until the people in power become humble
Common people of this earth will always stumble.

Emperors observing our precious lives tumble
What harms our existence never makes them crumble.

Their aid perpetuates our knack to fumble
Reducing our combined voice to a mumble.

Fueling the permanence of mind in jumble
Neglecting pertinent issues until we rumble.

Until the people in power become humble
Common people of this earth will always stumble.

\*

## *I Would Love to Love Me*
(C) 2007 Christopher A. Chaplin

It would be wonderful to love my mouth
But first I would have to learn how to talk
I could learn to talk like boys from down south
I be talking and singing as I walk.

I would be willing to love my two hands
If only I could control my fingers
They would audition for musical bands
Finger-puppet musicians and singers.

I would be willing to respect my feet
But I'd have to quit walking on my toes
I could be like Dad and strut down the street
Feet like leaves, traveling where the wind goes.

Autism is not easy on my mind
With love and friendships always hard to find.

\*

### *What It Is*
(C) 2006 Christopher A. Chaplin


Autism
Abnormal, Hungry
Creating, seeking, obsessing
Always fighting
Anxiety.


*

## *Admit It*
(C) 2006 Christopher A. Chaplin

"If you admit to yourself
What you are searching for
You'll be able to find it."

\*

## *Recognized For Change*
(C) 2006 Christopher A. Chaplin

"People do not change,
they are recognized for
what they've become at that moment."

\*

## *Mind Before Brain*
(C) 2006 Christopher A. Chaplin

"First created is the mind,
its purpose is to
deploy and find.
Second comes the brain,
its purpose is to
employ and retain."

*

## *Let Them Be Silly*
(C) 2006 Christopher A. Chaplin

"Let Them Be Silly
So They Can Become"

*

## *Roof Tree Sky Mountain*
(C) 2006 Christopher A. Chaplin

"If your ambitions are to reach for the
roof, you will learn how to climb a tree. If
 your ambitions are to reach for the sky,
then you will learn how to climb a mountain."

**\***

## *Embrace The Spirit*

(C) 2006 Christopher A. Chaplin

"If you seek the power
of your mind, then you must
first embrace the spirit
that you need to find it."

\*

# *Brain Problems Mind Solutions*

(C) 2006 Christopher A. Chaplin

"When we open up
our brains, we find
problems. When we
open up our minds,
we find solutions."

*

## *Box Others Circle Self*
(C) 2006 Christopher A. Chaplin

"If you want to attain your goals inside the box, then you will rely on the leverage of others.

If you want to attain your goals inside the circle, then you will rely on the momentum of your own will."

\*

## *Excuse Worth Living*
(C) 2006 Christopher A. Chaplin

"Keep trying, even if you
lose it all. At least you will
 have created a reason
to quit that you can live with."

*

# *Economize Mojo*
(C) 2006 Christopher A. Chaplin

"The cost of willpower isn't
free! Economize your mojo!"

*

## *No Cure For Leaves & Branches*
### (C) 2006 Christopher A. Chaplin

"If you practise taking care of the leaves, branches
 While neglecting to nurture the roots, how can you
Expect to discover, then cultivate a cure?"

\*

### *Mind Over Behaviors*
(C) 2006 Christopher A. Chaplin

"Our objective is to help the child attain a level
Of self-comprehension that will enable his mind to be-
Lieve that all behaviors exhibited are its decision."

\*

# *Lump Of Clay Like*

(C) 2007 Christopher A. Chaplin

An idea remains shapeless
Until its molding commences.

*

## *Surviving for Purpose*
(C) 2007 Christopher A. Chaplin

The miseries incurred while in pursuit of happiness
Are inflicted by the hands that induce our ambitions;
Validating our personal precious,
Justifying why we exist.

\*

## *Fiercer Becomes Enemy*
(C) 2006 Christopher A. Chaplin

"The closer we get
to our goals, the fiercer
The enemy grows."

*

### *Be Kind Mankind*
(C) 2006 Christopher A. Chaplin

"Spirit
has financed my
willpower; mankind must
finance the execution of
my plan."

\*

# *Pursue Willpower*
(C) 2006 Christopher A. Chaplin

"To develop the willpower to Pursue
a goal is to accept the consequences
for obtaining what you worked for."

*

# *Afraid Reaction*
### (C) 2006 Christopher A. Chaplin

"If you are afraid of the reaction,
Then you'll never commit to the action."

*

## *Autism To Some Degree*
(C) 2006 Christopher A. Chaplin

"Every human entity
Born with a disability, disorder, or disease
Experiences the effects of autism
To some degree."


*

## *Autism's Reality*
(C) 2006 Christopher A. Chaplin

"We can eradicate the outward effects of autism,
We can never completely remove anxiety itself."

\*

## Self Generator
(C) 2006 Christopher A. Chaplin

"Find the desire and you
Will generate willpower."

\*

## *Seek & Find*

(C) 2006 Christopher A. Chaplin

"To find
Anxiety,
We must apply pressure.
To lose anxiety, remove
Pressure."

*

## *Like the Wind*
(C) 2006 Christopher A. Chaplin

"Autism is like the wind;
it is invisible. You
can see its effects, but you
can't see autism itself."

\*

# *Encouragement Stories* ©

These **Encouragement Stories** ©, while very "personal," are written in a manner to impart a lesson and to aid parents of physically, mentally, and emotionally challenged children to cope with the situations they face. I am not saying that my way is the way, but rather, "Here are examples to help caregivers to 'imagine' coping mechanisms that will work specifically for their child."

The *"Yeah We Did It!"* **Encouragement Stories** © offer parents, caregivers, educators, and therapists unique insights into the management of developmentally challenged children from the perspective on a hands-on parent who must continually seek unconventional means to help his child overcome the difficulties of the condition.

Parents of developmentally challenged children (who have medical and/or psychological diagnoses) need behavior management tools that are practical and supportive. A child's picture book can be not only a fun and inspirational way to assist the parents with improving their child's learning and social skills, but also a way to help instill confidence in the child.

*"Yeah We Did It!"* is a series of short **Encouragement Stories** © that I have developed. The **Encouragement Stories** © follow the life of a developmentally challenged boy, highlighting the various obstacles to his learning abilities, celebrating his achievements, and underlining the role that his parents take in helping him.

Throughout these **Encouragement Stories** © and those planned for the entire series, Christopher asks difficult questions that are familiar to parents of special needs children. Dad answers them honestly and uses ("whatever works") unusual learning props to help explain everything.

# We're Going To Do It
## ISBN 978-1-897347-07-2

# *We're Going To Do It*

Christopher A. Chaplin
Illustrated by Teodora Sirko

*We're Going To Do It* sets the stage for this uniquely expressed series of child development stories. Mom and Dad rush to the hospital and give birth to a bi-racial boy named Christopher. Mom and Dad's dreams are shattered when they receive news from the doctor that their son was born with hemophilia, a severe bleeding disorder. The bills pile to the ceiling and Mom is forced to go back to work. Dad stays home and takes care of Christopher, who is not developing like most other children. Stress on the family forces Mom and Dad to separate. Christopher begins to exhibit many unusual behaviors and is diagnosed with a Neurological disorder. All hope seems lost for Christopher, but Dad decides to not give up and vows to help Christopher manage his challenges.

**Reviewed by**: A.LaRocque-Rooney ECE, CYW, DSW

A well written "True to life" of what happens to most couples who learn that their child may not be what most call "typical". The story "We Are Going To Do It!" deals with situations many parents of Autistic children may encounter. The illustrations are full of life and color, and detailed enough to create conversation with children who listen to, and read this story over and over again.

I had the opportunity to share this well written book with young children who have autism and the response is very positive and requested reading time and again.

A.LaRocque-Rooney ECE, CYW, DSW

**Reviewed by**: Jody Felske Intermediate Teacher (Teacher)

We're Going to do It! is a wonderful, inspiring story of new parents learning of their first child's dual diagnosis of hemophilia and autism. The author, Chris Chaplin, shares the strife and sorrow that accompanied this personal situation, and lends encouragement to other parents who may face similar difficulties. This book also serves as an effective vehicle through which children's questions about these two conditions can be delicately answered.

Through creative descriptions (Nurse Prick-Helps, Dr. Fix-Your-Head) and dynamic illustrations, the story invites the reader to learn about what little Christopher has to deal with, along with his parents. This book would be a wonderful addition to any home or school library, with its meaningful story and rich, lively language.

Jody Felske Intermediate Teacher (Toronto District School Board)

**Reviewed by**: Frances Savella Honours BSc, BEd, Specialist in Special Education Teacher Toronto District School Board

We're Going To Do It is a heart-warming, true account of a couples struggle with the acceptance that their new baby boy has been dually diagnosed with Autism and Hemophilia. Feeling the financial and emotional strain, dad and mom decide to separate and dad takes primary care of Christopher who visits his mom regularly. Christopher's self-abusive behaviours, lack of emotional connectedness, sensory issues, fears of people and open spaces and reluctance to touch becomes the driving force that propels dad to use Christopher's gifts to work diligently and relentlessness in allowing Christopher to live a joyful, fearless and wholesome existence. This is a must read! It is a testimonial that all one needs to make a difference is love, determination and an unrelentless will to beat the odds. This heartfelt story will touch your heart and inspire encouragement and faith!

Frances Savella Honours BSc, BEd, Specialist in Special Education Teacher Toronto District School Board

Tara Stephen (teacher). says

"Christopher A. Chaplin has filled a niche for the parents, siblings, teachers, caregivers and classmates of special needs children. It was a joy to stumble onto picture books that clearly explain and creatively illustrate the perspective of parent and child. The world of autism, ADHD and other diagnoses can challenge and baffle those who come in contact with them each day. Chaplin's stories are written in such a way as to allow the reader to gently enter this unique world. They are a comfortable read-aloud with plenty of opportunity for discussion at the level of the listener.

# Boing! Boing! Boing!

## *Boing! Boing! Boing!*

Christopher A. Chaplin
Illustrated by Teodora Sirko

*Boing! Boing! Boing!* shows a shut-down and withdrawn Christopher who is non-active and uninterested in exploring places, discovering things, and interacting with people like other girls and boys his age. Dad is forced to take his son outside in the nighttime but continues to teach him about the things they see and the sounds they hear. Christopher only wants to hide his face and block his ears in fear. By chance, Dad stops in to see the storekeeper who gives him some candy drops that he promises will give Christopher "the hops." By using the candy as a special type of learning tool, Dad helps Christopher to become interested in people, places, and things.

# Motor Mouth

# *Motor Mouth*

Christopher A. Chaplin
Illustrated by Teodora Sirko

*Motor Mouth* is about a little boy who has trouble speaking and finds it difficult to initiate speech. Christopher wants to talk with other children but becomes embarrassed and violent when his mouth won't let his words come out. Dad visits Mr. Storekeeper, who supplies Dad with a few treats (edible and otherwise) that will help to exercise Christopher's mouth muscles. A fierce blizzard attacks the town and Christopher and Dad are snowed in, inside their apartment where they spend the whole winter playing speech and language learning games, chewing bubblegum, blowing up balloons, and popping sunflower seeds in their mouths. Dad finds ways to manage his son's anxiety, Christopher's mouth begins to motor, and words are finally able to spill out.

# Finding Squeezey

## *Finding Squeezey*

Christopher A. Chaplin
Illustrated by Diana McManus Whitman

*Finding Squeezey* is the story of a little boy who is usually afraid of strange people, places, and things. Christopher's anxiety around other children makes him self-injurious and it very difficult for him to grow and learn. He must also cope with weekly trips to the hospital to receive the medication he needs to control his hemophilia. Christopher explains that he needs something to make him feel safe when Dad isn't holding him. Dad and Christopher search the Daddy-I-Want-It department store for something that Christopher can use as a "special friend" that will keep him safe.

Unexpectedly Christopher stumbles upon a huge green fluffy towel that will be the very thing he needs. Christopher names the towel Squeezey because of way the towel wraps around and hugs him. Soon after getting Squeezey, Christopher begins to get more comfortable with being around others.

# Inside Tubsy

# *Inside Tubsy*

Christopher A. Chaplin
Illustrated by Diana McManus Whitman

*Inside Tubsy* confronts Christopher's fear of water. Dad uses the green fluffy towel named Squeezey as a bridge and to give his son a sense of security. The bathtub eventually becomes a safe haven for Christopher, who now continues his development and learns to confront his anxieties and triumph over his fears.

# Say Bump Me

# *Say Bump Me*

Christopher A. Chaplin
Illustrated by Diana McManus Whitman

*Say Bump Me* addresses the difficulty that developmentally challenged children have when meeting other children. Christopher wants to make friends, but whenever he attempts to do so, his anxiety takes over and causes him to exhibit violent tantrums. Dad convinces him to use one of his pet expressions, "Bump me," (and offering the knuckles of his hand to "bump" the knuckles of the other person) as a way to break the ice when meeting new people. Christopher learns to use "Bump me" as a way to successfully relieve this particular anxiety.

# Losing Squeezey

# *Losing Squeezey*

Christopher A. Chaplin
Illustrated by Diana McManus Whitman

*Losing Squeezey* shows how an object often provides emotional security for a child who has medical or psychological challenges. In this story, Christopher expresses anxiety when Squeezey is lost. Christopher grows increasingly angry and will not eat, learn, or socialize without his special towel. The story culminates with Dad and Christopher's successful search to find Squeezey.

# Squeezey Wonders

# *Squeezey Wonders*

Christopher A. Chaplin
Illustrated by Diana McManus Whitman

*Squeezey Wonders* is the tale of what happens to Squeezey when she becomes separated from Christopher and is taken to a scary warehouse. Squeezey worries that she will never see Christopher again and endures the harrowing experience of being used by many different people for many different reasons. When all hope seems lost, Squeezey is reunited with Christopher.

# Owl Eyes

# *Owl Eyes*

Christopher A. Chaplin
Illustrated by Teodora Sirko

*Owl Eyes* is the story of how Dad helps Christopher overcome socializing difficulties by learning to make eye contact with things and people. Christopher struggles with communicating and how to understand his surroundings, thus making him insecure and unwilling to socialize with other people. Dad takes him to "Explanation Park" for a hike, and helps Christopher to gain a new perspective on making eye contact with people, places, and things. This helps Christopher to be more receptive to experiencing life through learning and interaction.

# Boof

# *Boof*

Christopher A. Chaplin
Illustrated by Diana McManus Whitman

*Boof* is a humorous way of exploring the serious issues that parents of self-injurious children encounter. Christopher gives reasons for his behavior, and Dad takes him to see a wizard to get a remedy. Christopher is given learning incentives and develops a stronger self-identity. He stops "Boofing" his head. The plot is a fun fantasy that tickles the senses.

# Yeah, I Love Mommy Today

## *Yeah, I Love Mommy Today*

Christopher A. Chaplin
Illustrated by Teodora Sirko

*Yeah, I Love Mommy Today* explains the difficulties that separated parents and their children experience during parental visitations. Christopher is happily living with Dad and has trouble handling the change in routine when it is time to visit his mother. Dad prepares Christopher to see his mother, who has made special plans for their day together. Christopher and Mom are about to leave when their plans to go to Explanation Park come suddenly to a halt. Christopher begins to tantrum, Mom panics, and calls Dad, who gives her an activity that will help to calm Christopher. Mom develops a stronger bond with her son and Christopher now says "Yeah! I love Mommy today!" every time he goes to visit her.

# Babble

# *Babble*

Christopher A. Chaplin
Illustrated by Teodora Sirko

*Babble* shows how parents of special needs children must sometimes endure public embarrassment caused by inappropriate behavior by their children. Christopher has overcome many hurdles and is ready to meet the world. However, each time he catches someone's attention, he begins to "babble" his life story. Christopher's newly learned skill of socializing is complicated by his inability to relate well to others, which makes him anxious when social interactions do not go his way. Christopher hikes to Explanation Park where he stumbles upon the answers he needs while sitting underneath the "Question Tree."

# Mommy Says It's a Monster

## *Mommy Says It's a Monster*

Christopher A. Chaplin
Illustrated by Teodora Sirko

*Mommy Says It's A Monster* is an action-packed piece that explores the difficulties that parents have when trying to explain to their developmentally challenged children the difference between real and make believe. Christopher and Dad are stuck in their car during an angry thunderstorm, and are unable to get home. Christopher is about to throw a tantrum because he doesn't believe that "the monster" is a "storm" (verbalizing the different terms that Mom and Dad use, respectively). Dad uses different strategies to help Christopher differentiate between real and make believe and Christopher's speech and language become increasingly more rational.

# Act Alive and Say High-Five

## *Act Alive and Say High-Five*

Christopher A. Chaplin
Illustrated by Teodora Sirko

Most parents of shy children need behavior management tools that are practical and supportive. A child's picture book can not only be a fun and inspirational way to assist the caregivers with improving their children's learning and social skills, but also a way to encourage confidence in the child.

*Act Alive and Say High-Five* is a giggly way to address the difficulty that shy children may experience when meeting other children. The little girl wants to say hello, but whenever she attempts to do so, she looks up at her father and says "I want to go home." Dad comforts his daughter and then "smack" go their hands as Dad gives his little girl an unexpected high-five. "What was that for?" asks the little girl. "That is your new way to say hello. The next time you feel shy, Just Act Alive and Say High-Five," Dad explains.

The little girl questions her father and does not believe saying hello can be so easy, but soon must put her newfound way to the test. She spots a boy coming toward her and begins to feel uneasy. Dad gives his daughter a quick pep talk and she is prepared to "Act Alive and Say High-Five."

# Bodola
## ISBN 978-1-897347-04-1

# *Bodola*

Christopher A. Chaplin
Illustrated by Teodora Sirko

*Bodola* is a cheerful, adventurous story that shows the difficult decisions parents of children diagnosed with Down Syndrome, A.D.H.D or PDD are forced to make as their busy and spontaneous mid-graders begin to manifest their desires for independence.

Like most boys and girls, Bodola is a boy who enjoys jiving, singing, playing with toys, and, most of all, he loves chips and pop. He's never been to the store by himself, and he asks Mama to please let him go today. Mama knows that Bodola gets excited by new things and tends to forget what he is doing, but she wants him to learn about the responsibility that comes with being independent. While on his way to the store, he embarks on an adventure of riding a train and then a bus, and is delighted by the sights he sees along the way. Mama attempts desperately to catch up to her son before he realizes that he didn't do what Mama told him to do and panics.

*Bodola* is crafted by an experienced parent/independent researcher with the intention to optimize the reading experience and enable its audience to obtain a fuller comprehension of Obsessive-Compulsive Disorder (intrusive thinking) and associated theories of the mind that will, in turn, empower readers to self-regulate the development of deleterious behaviors.

**Reviewed by**: Dr. Bob Rich
**Publisher**: MasterpieceFactory Inc.

This beautifully illustrated book automatically attracts the attention to little children. The story line is inherently entertaining for them, and will get frequent chuckles from the adult reading it for the small child. However, this is far more than the usual kids' picture book. Without ever lecturing, it provides a model for how to treat a child who is not (or not yet) capable of exercising self-discipline and restraint. When the rather oddly named little boy Bodola causes his mother endless worry and inconvenience, she reacts without anger or abuse, but rather corrects the situation and uses gentle corrective action to teach her son the lesson he needs. Patience and love are used instead of harsh discipline.

I have no criticism of this lovely little addition to any home library.

**Reviewed by**: Jody Felske (Teacher)
**Publisher**: MasterpieceFactory Inc.

Bodola is a fun and cheery story that illustrates some of the difficulties that a mother and her child that has attention deficits and compulsive behaviours face. Bodola wants more than anything to go to the store on his own like his peers do, and when his mother finally allows this, a possibly dangerous adventure ensues. The author captures Bodola's mother's anxiety in dealing with the situation, and offers a solution to the problem as well.

Once again, the author/art director, along with illustrator Teodora Sirko, has come up with rich illustrations with which children and parents can extrapolate. The ending of this story leaves the reader wondering what adventures Bodola might find himself partaking in next, as surely will be found in Chaplin's future books.

Jody Felske Intermediate Teacher (Toronto District School Board)

**Reviewed by**: Frances Savella Honours BSc, BEd, Specialist in Special Education Teacher Toronto District School Board

Bodola: Chips & Pop is a creatively written and illustrated story of a boy with ADHD/ Autism who embarks on an adventure of independence to buy his favorite snack; chips and pop. This beautifully crafted story captures the essence of what many children with ADHD experience; navigating through a world saturated with sounds, sights, smells, tastes and textures while concurrently dealing with preoccupations and preservations that can hold a child with ADHD prisoner. This inspiring story appeals to adults and children alike and teaches very important lessons of tolerance, acceptance and determination. Bodola: Chips and Pop clearly shows that with understanding and perseverance, we can all overcome our weaknesses.

**Comments**

Tara Stephen (teacher). says

"Christopher A. Chaplin has filled a niche for the parents, siblings, teachers, caregivers and classmates of special needs children. It was a joy to stumble onto picture books that clearly explain and creatively illustrate the perspective of parent and child. The world of autism, ADHD and other diagnoses can challenge and baffle those who come in contact with them each day. Chaplin's stories are written in such a way as to allow the reader to gently enter this unique world. They are a comfortable read-aloud with plenty of opportunity for discussion at the level of the listener.

Sharing from his own experiences, Chaplin's books are an invaluable educational tool for families and teachers trying to understand the difficulties these precious little ones may encounter in a seemingly ordinary daily routine. Every school, daycare and doctors office should have copies as a gentle way to inform and educate adults, and to sensitively answer the questions of children."

Tara Stephen
-Literacy Co-ordinator & Elementary Teacher with Toronto District School Board
-President of Centennial Child Care Centre Board of Directors
- Mother of three

Joey Anthony Perreault (Boy, 9 Years Old, ADHD). says

"I think that your book was great! I have ADHD so it is hard for me to remember stuff like that im exited all the time I love reading and I love your book and I thank you for sending your book to me and my mom thank you bye."

A.LaRocque-Rooney ECE, CYW, DSW. says

This is the story of Bodola, who finds himself on an adventure filled with bright images of the world. This book, like others from the author, is well written with captivating illustrations. Parents will find many topics of conversation to explore with their child, and many lessons to share.

A.LaRocque-Rooney, ECE, CYW, DSW

# *Egg Chip*

Christopher A. Chaplin
Illustrated by Diana M. Whitman

In Egg Chip Christopher displays the fastidious behaviors of autism that make it difficult for him to move past the slightest change. The boy meets Change-gee the Clown at Explanation Park and finds out about inconsistencies, choices, and consequences. Christopher encounters many people doing things in many different ways during a train ride to Diverse-City, and learns to accept the differences that the world presents.

## Mr. I-Presume
## Visits Planet Earth

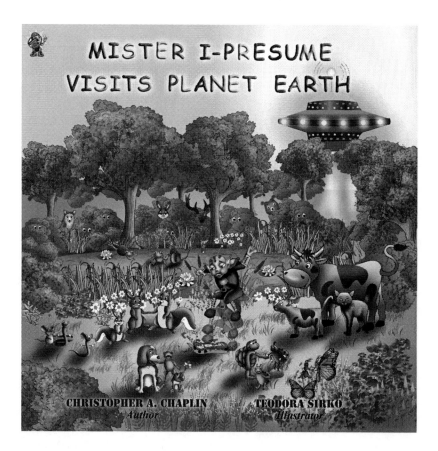

# Mr. I-Presume
# Visits Planet Earth

## Christopher A. Chaplin
## Illustrated by Teodora Sirko

*Mr. I-Presume* underlines the essence of this delightfully crafted social lesson that things are not always as they seem. During this whimsically expressed story, an alien, suitably named Mr. I-Presume, is excited at the opportunity to visit the forgotten planet known as Earth. He packs his trusted special phone that stores "The Book of Beliefs" information about the planet to help identify whatever he discovers while there.

The spaceship lands and Mr. I-Presume begins to walk along a wooded road where he spots a life form that is inside a soggy log and chewing on a bone. He quickly refers to the display on his phone to learn about the look and sound of what he thinks is a funky furry rat. Mr. I-Presume says hello to the strange being. Instead of hearing Screech! Screech! like the sound most rats make, the rat actually begins to Rib-bit! Rib-Bit! like a frog.

The alien scratches his tentacles and continues his exploration of our silly planet Earth. He explores Earth and comes across many beings that are not as what he was led to believe, according to "The Book of Beliefs." Mr. I-Presume wants to escape these topsy-turvy beings and sends a transmission to his home planet, Peaches and Cream, requesting a spaceship to beam him home. He has discovered that, on Earth, things are not always as they seem.

# Tipee-Toe Tony & Mr. One-Hand

## Tipee-Toe Tony & Mr. One-Hand

Christopher A. Chaplin
Illustrated by Nicholas Write

In this fast-moving, easy-reading mid-grade Explore & Discover picture story, a grimy young man named Tipee-Toe Tony and his scruffy puppy, Gruffy, live in a dented oil drum located in a vacant parking lot that everybody calls Hobo City.

Tipee-Toe Tony finds himself in a desperate mood as he and Gruffy are starving for food when, just like that, Tipee-Toe Tony has a plan and decides to tap dance and beat the top of his dented can like a drum, with the hope of filling his tin cup with money to buy some much-needed ham and jam to fry in his pan. Sure enough, after tap dancing and beating on his drum, Tipee-Toe Tony attracts a man with one hand who wants to give the grimy young man some money--if Tipee-Toe will give the man his right hand.

Tipee-Toe thinks about all his dreams, as well as his immediate need for food, and wonders if he would be better off with a pocket full of money and only one hand. Will Tipee-Toe Tony decide to sacrifice his hand for his immediate needs, or will he think about his future and refuse to sell his hand to the stranger?

# Tipee-Toe Tony Goes To Strawberry City

## *Tipee-Toe Tony Goes To Strawberry City*

Christopher A. Chaplin
Illustrated by Nicholas Write

Hip, Hip Hooray! Tipee-Toe Tony is moving out of Hobo City today. In this mid-grade Explore & Discover picture story, the grimy young man and his scruffy puppy, Gruffy, pack their bag full of ham and jam and are immediately faced with choices and consequences on their long journey to see his friend Fussy Sam who lives in Strawberry City.

Tipee-Toe Tony and Gruffy walk for miles and become angry, hungry, and tired. After a quick meal, Tipee-Toe Tony and Gruffy continue their journey when they are stopped by a sobbing young girl and her Daddy in a red truck along the roadside. The man informs the Tipee-Toe Tony that the only way he can reach Strawberry City before nightfall by foot is to cut through Spooky Forest where an assortment of wild and scary animals, including a vicious wolf known as Nasty Fangs, are waiting to eat him.

The man offers Tipee-Toe Tony a ride in his truck in exchange for his loyal puppy, Gruffy. Tipee-Toe Tony has his mind set on reaching Strawberry City before nightfall and contemplates giving his canine companion away to the man's crying little girl. Will Tipee-Toe Tony give up Gruffy and travel with the stranger? Or will Tipee-Toe Tony attempt to sneak through Spooky Forest and avoid being eaten by Nasty Fangs?

## Spooky Forest

### *Spooky Forest*

Christopher A. Chaplin
Illustrated by Nicholas Write

Like most teenage boys, Tipee-Toe Tony cannot resist a good adventure. In this story, the grimy young man places his life in danger by stuffing Gruffy, his puppy, in his backpack and boldly riding his bike through Spooky Forest in hopes of reaching Strawberry City before sunset.

During their long bumpy bike ride, they begin to hear threatening sounds of forest creatures, notice paw prints along the forest floor, and see claw-marked trees that crowd the dark damp path as they attempt to sneak through Spooky Forest. Tipee-Toe Tony and Gruffy decide to stop and fry some ham and jam, but the smoke from their fire wafts through the forest and arouses Nasty fangs and his pack of furious friends.

Nasty Fangs is only a few yards away when a boy named Spooky Duke appears and leads Tipee-Toe Tony and Gruffy along a fallen tree to the edge of a steep cliff where they are forced to make a decision between leaping off or sharing the same sad consequence as all who had ever dared to attempt to travel through Spooky Forest. How are Tipee-Toe Tony and Gruffy going to escape this time?

## Mr. I-Presume & Friends
## Picture Story Coloring Book
## ISBN 978-1-897347-01-0

## *Mr. I-Presume & Friends*
## *Picture Story Coloring Book*

Christopher A. Chaplin
Illustrated by Pamela Masi


*Mr. I-Presume & Friends* is a whimsical interactive Explore & Discovery © Picture Story that entertains while it stimulates growth in all areas of child development for both typical and developmentally challenged children. In this early reading adventure, Mr. I-Presume beams down to planet Earth and introduces his audience to his family and unique friends.

Mr. I-Presume advances speech & language, comprehension, and perceptual motor skills in many ways such as teaching readers how to say "Hip, Hip, Hooray!" and "Good-bye" in the Alien language, duplicated uncolored pages, funny looking creatures with silly names, as well as further stimulating readers with story-related questions and fill-in-the blanks exercises.

*Mr. I-Presume & Friends* is a fun learning tool that will encourage desirable mental growth, and empower children to independently observe and interpret information about their own world.

# Samples Of My Soul

*A Mind-opening Collection Of Fresh Expressive Poetry and HeadItchies (c).*

By Christopher A. Chaplin

## Coming Christmas 2007

A Poetry Book about pursuing, procuring and becoming your life's purpose, existing with autism, anxiety, depression, the abstract aspects of love and life.

## Join Our Forum
read our poems and Encouragement Stories
## For Free

## About The Author

**Christopher A. Chaplin** was born in August 1970, and grew up in the west side of Toronto, Ontario, Canada in a slummy metro housing unit that is still nestled within the upper middle-class village of Swansea.

Being the first born of three children (Christopher, one brother and one sister) who were raised single-handedly by their Jamaica-born mother, Christopher's quest for freedom from the hustle of the ghetto inspired him to gain knowledge through work experience such as delivering newspapers at the age of 11 to becoming a trend-setting entrepreneur in the pet food industry during the early 1990s. Despite his positive goals, Christopher struggled with anxiety and depression until he finally stumbled upon his purpose and learned to express himself through writing, primarily in the form of children's literature.

Christopher is a single parent of a child dually diagnosed with autism and hemophilia. He also has two older daughters. He graduated in 2005 as an Early Childhood Assistant and is, independently, studying child psychology and children's literature. Christopher is dedicated to bringing to light the positive aspects of parenting children who have special needs. Looking back at past desires, the author says, "I have always been fascinated by the power of a good book."

Christopher began his professional writing career in the early 1990s when he was encouraged to create commercial pieces such as monthly newsletters, flyers, and press releases for the pet food delivery service he was involved with at the time.

He is a self-taught writer who possesses a refreshing enthusiasm to learn and continues to experiment with new ways of expressing his unique stories, which are not only engaging children's stories, but also tools for acquiring life skills. His mission is to motivate other individuals to think positively about whatever challenges they might face in their lives.

Christopher founded MasterpieceFactory Inc. as an outlet for his work and especially to empower readers to develop their own ideas and solutions for parenting developmentally challenged children or who suffer from other diseases, disabilities, or disorders.

*

Photo by Zell Ers